Grade **1.2**

Scott Foresman

Decodable Practice Readers 7A - 18C
Volume 2
Units 2 and 3

Scott Foresman
is an imprint of

PEARSON

Glenview, Illinois • Boston, Massachusetts • Chandler, Arizona
• Upper Saddle River, New Jersey

ISBN-13: 978-0-328-49215-2
ISBN-10:   0-328-49215-9
12 13 14 15   V011   17 16 15 14 13
CC1

Contents

Fishing with Tad

Written by Sandra Demnik

Consonant Digraph _th_/th/

thin   thick

Consonant Digraph _th_/ᵮH/

with   this   that
them   then

Consonant Digraph _sh_/sh/

shack   fish
shut

Initial Consonant Blends

stop   plop

Final Consonant Blends

pond   best

Inflected Ending _-ing_

fishing   renting

High-Frequency Words

the	I	go
one	said	put
into	a	

1

Tad is with his mom
and dad at the pond.

Tad has his thin rod.
"I can go fishing with this."

Dad stops at the best shack.
"Dad is renting that one,"
Mom said.

Dad and Mom get fish.
"Put them into this thick box.
Shut the lid."

Tad is sad.
Mom has fish.
Dad has fish.

Then Tad tugs and tugs.
It is big!

Tad tugs and then plop!
This is not a fish!

Get the Ball

Written by Christina Potter

Vowel Sound in *ball: a, al*

ball	talk	walk
call	small	tall

Consonant *k*

walk   talk

Initial Consonant Blends

stuck   small   step

High-Frequency Words

the	are	tree
they	to	

Hit the ball, Ben.
Ben can not hit it.

Hit the ball, Nick.
Nick hits the ball.

It is stuck in that tree.

Ben and Nick are small.
They can not get it.

Call Tim.
Can Tim get the ball?
Tim can not get the ball.

Walk up and talk to Mom.
Mom is tall.

Mom can step up and get the ball.
Hit the ball, Mom.

A Plan for Trash

Written by Josh Grober

Consonant Digraph _sh_

fish   shack   trash

Consonant Digraph _th_/th/

thin   path

Consonant Digraph _th_/Ŧh/

this   that   with   them

Vowel Sound in _ball_: _a, al_

ball   walk   talk   all   call

High-Frequency Words

a   to   the

my   good

Let us get this ball.

That is not fun at all.

Let us get a fish at that thin shack.

I can not walk to the shack and back.

Let us call Brad and Jim
and talk with them.

That is not my plan.

Let us pick up the trash on the path.
That plan is good!

Kate Wins the Game

Written by Moira McGinty

Long *a*: *a_e*

Kate	brave	save	makes
waves	take	shakes	Flames
Jane	Dale	game	
late	lake	shade	

Consonant Digraph *sh*/sh/

shade   smash

High-Frequency Words

the	to	her	you
do	a		

Kate can kick the ball.

Mom and Dad take Kate
to her game.
Kate waves to them.

Dale kicks the ball to the shade.
Jane kicks it in the lake.

Dad calls, "You can do it, Kate!"
Mom yells, "Run, Kate, run!"

Kate makes a late kick.
The ball is in the net!

Kate and her smash kick save
the game.
The Flames win!

Mom calls Kate brave.
Dad shakes her hand.

Where Is Dave?

Written by John Parquette

Decodable Practice Reader

8B

Consonant c/s/

race
lace
place
face

Consonant g/j/

cage

Long a: a_e

Dave   cage   race   take
lace   place   face

Vowel Sound in ball: a, al

walk   ball

Initial Consonant Blends

steps   black   place

High-Frequency Words

where   the   my
a   here   go

Dave is not in his cage.
Where is Dave?

Is Dave on the steps?
Did Dave race up the walk?

Did Dave take my black ball?
Where is it?

Is Dave in bed?
Did Dave get this sock?

This had a lace.
Where did it go?

Is Dave in this place?
Is that his face?

Dave jumps up.
Yes, Dave is here!

Jane Can Race

Written by Peter Penn

Consonant c/s/

face   race

Consonant g/j/

cage   age

Long a: a_e

Jane	ape	face
name	snake	cage
cave	race	
age	wave	
gate	take	

High-Frequency Words

the	like	look
a	they	

41

Jane can make an ape face.

Jane can name the big cats.

Jane can talk like the snake
in that cage.

Jane can look in that cave.
A cub is in it.

Jane can race with the ducks.
They can not run fast at this age.

Jane can wave at the gate.

Jane can take a nap on the bus.

The Bike

Written by Erika Ullmann

Long i: i_e

Mike	hike	twice	like	size
nice	mine	fine	bike	side
times	rides	hide	five	smiles

Initial Consonant Blends

small   twice   smiles   black

High-Frequency Words

a	wants	your	he
said	to	no	my
the	what		

Mike rides a small bike.
But he wants a nice big bike.

Mike tells Mom twice.
He tells Dad five times.

"Your bike is just fine,"
Dad said to Mike.

"No, it is not my size,"
Mike said to Dad.

Dad and Mike hike to the shed.
What did Dad hide at the side?

Mike yells, "Is it mine?"
"Like it?" Dad asks.

Dad smiles.
Mike hugs Dad and his big
black bike.

Catch the Bus

Written by Mary Brenton

Consonant Digraphs *wh, ch, -tch, ph*

which	catch	checks	graph	white
such	when	pitch	chips	

Long *i: i_e*

times	line	ride	white	nice

Consonant *c/s/*

nice	place

High-Frequency Words

to	the	I	for
a	put	go	

57

Mom and Pam walk to the bus stop.

Which bus can Mom and Pam catch?
Mom checks the graph for times.

Mom and Pam get in line
and then ride the bus.

"Can I get this red and white cap?
It is such a nice fit.
I can put it on when I pitch."

Pam has chips.
Mom gets the check.

When will Mom and Pam go back to that place?

It is time to catch the bus.

Which Job?

Written by Margaret Ronzarie

We all like to help.
Which jobs are on the graph?

Peg can make ice.

Dad can chop and mix.
Dad made too much rice.

Mom can fix this latch.

Chip can place trash
in sacks and get rid of it.

Champ can chase and fetch.

We did the jobs.
It is time for fun!

A Note for Rose

Written by Seline Baxter

Long *o*: *o_e*

note	those	Rose	bone
hope	rope	stove	home

Syllable Pattern VCe

make	Kate	take	note
Rose	hope	stove	those
bone	rope	home	gave

High-Frequency Words

a	I	to	her	working
put	go	where	here	

73

Mom will make a snack.
"I must get nuts."

"Kate, take this note to Rose.
I hope Rose has nuts."

Rose is working at her stove.
"Take those nuts, Kate, and
put them in this sack."
Rose hands Max a bone.

Jan is jumping rope.
"Can I jump?" asks Kate.

"I must go home."
"Where is that sack?" Jan asks.

"Here it is. Max has it."

"Mom, Rose gave us nuts and
a bone."

I'm Glad

Written by Hanna Fross

Contractions

didn't	isn't	I'm
can't	it'll	

Syllable Pattern VCe

rides	bikes	safe
place	fine	
came	smiles	

High-Frequency Words

the	want	to	a
I	be	we	going

81

Tom rides bikes with Mike and Dad.
Mike and Dad ride up the hill.

Tom didn't want to ride up it.

Dad calls to Tom.
"It isn't a big hill."

"Ride up it, Tom," calls Dad.
"I'm going as fast as I can."

"That path has rocks on it.
It can't be a safe place to ride."

"We can walk back. It'll be fine."

"I'm glad we came," Tom smiles.
"This is fun."

Isn't This Fun?

Written by Chris Arvetis

Contractions	Long o: o_e	
it'll	woke	hope
I'm	drove	hole
isn't	close	
didn't	those	
can't		

High-Frequency Words

I	come	to	you
the	we		

89

Jim woke up.
"I hope it'll get hot."

"Can Tim and Rob come with us?
I'm calling them."

Mom drove us to the lake.

Jim and Tim dig.
This hole isn't big yet.

"We came to swim, didn't we?"
asks Rob.

"You can't wade close to those rocks," Mom calls.

It is fun at the lake.

June and Pete

Written by Fran Jacobs

Long *u: u_e*

June   mule   huge   rude   use

Long *e: e_e*

Pete   Steve

Consonant g/j/

age   huge

Long *o: o_e*

hopes   home   votes

High-Frequency Words

here   to   go   be
there   too   the

97

Here is June.
June is age six and small.
June hopes to go home.

Here is Pete the mule.
Pete is huge.
Pete can help June.

June can ride on Pete
to get there.

But Pete is
rude to June.
It makes June sad.

Pete gave this to June.
June will not be sad.

Pete takes June to Steve the frog.
Can Steve ride too?
June votes yes!

Steve hops on Pete.
June and Steve use Pete
to get home.

Luke Meets Pete

Written by Elizabeth Hawkins

Inflected Ending -ed

asked   looked   added
called   walked

Long e: e_e

Gene   Pete

Long u: u_e

Luke   dune
June   cute
mule   cubes

High-Frequency Words

a   said   looked
eat   be   she

Luke sat at his home
on a dune at Lake Gene.

June came with a cute mule.
Luke asked his name.

"His name is Pete," June said.
"Pete is a fine mule."

Pete looked at Luke.
"Pete likes Luke,"
June added.

"Can Pete eat with us?"
Luke asked.
"It will be fun!"

"Pete!" June called.
Pete walked fast.
Pete looked glad.

"Pete eats cubes,"
June said.
She gave Pete his cubes.

112

Cubes, Rules, and Tunes

Written by John Roberts

Long *u: u_e*

June	cube
cute	Luke
tune	flute
rules	

Long *e: e_e*

Zeke	these

Inflected Ending *-ed*

asked	looked

High-Frequency Words

a	look	the

113

"Can June make a cube?"
Zeke asked.

June made a cube.
June has a cute cube.

June asked, "Can Luke
name a tune?"

Luke can name a tune.
It is a flute tune.

Luke asked, "Can Zeke
look at the game rules?"

Zeke looked at these rules
in his box.

Luke, June, and Zeke
had fun!

Dee, Lee, and the Green Plants

Written by Tim Stevens

Decodable
Practice
Reader
12A

Long e: e

she	be	we

Long e: ee

Dee	seeds	needs	Lee
feeds	weeds	weeks	see
green	three	wheels	need
tree	beets	sweet	free

Consonant Digraph th/th/

thin	three

Consonant Digraph th/ᵺh/

then	these

Consonant Digraph wh/wh/

when	wheels

High-Frequency Words

puts	little	the	work
for	they	many	to
under	a	are	said

Dee digs holes.
She puts in thin little seeds.
Lee helps when she needs it.

Lee feeds the plants.
Then he picks the weeds.
Dee helps.

Lee and Dee work for weeks.
They see many tall green plants.

Dee and Lee use this box.
It has three wheels.

Lee and Dee need to rest.
They sit under a tree.

Dee and Lee pick beets.
These beets will be sweet.
And they are free!

"We did it!" said Lee and Dee.

Bandit

Written by Renee Johnson

Syllables VC/CV

Bandit   kitten   rabbits   basket

Long e: e

he   we   be   she   me

Long e: ee

three   meet   tree   sleep

High-Frequency Words

my	was	old	to
the	a	now	they
together	do	food	

Bandit is my pup.
He was three weeks old
when we got him.

Dad and Mom like Bandit.
He is small, but he will be big.

Bandit ran to meet the kitten.
She ran up a tree.

Now she likes Bandit.
They sleep together.

Bandit likes rabbits,
but rabbits do not
like him.

Bandit likes jumping
up on me.
Mom gave Bandit food.

Bandit sleeps
in his black basket.
His bed is soft.

A Rabbit and a Kitten

Written by Dorothy Johnson

Dee has a basket.
It is deep and green.

Dee keeps a small rabbit
in this basket.

Rabbit is black, but she
has white feet.

Rabbit is a sweet pet.
Dee likes her.

Dee has a kitten too.
He is tan.

Kitten likes to be with Rabbit.

Dee has nice pets.
They like the basket.

Can Billy Fly?

Written by Rob Knight

Vowel Sound of *y*: /ī/

my	why	fly	trying
cry	by	try	sky

Vowel Sound of *y*: /ē/

silly	Billy	funny	Dotty
sunny	Freddy	happy	

Contractions

isn't	don't
can't	

Syllables VC/VC

rabbit	happen
contest	

High-Frequency Words

wants	to	a	the
what	you	are	

Meet my silly rabbit.
Why is Billy silly?
He wants to fly.

Billy is trying to fly.
Bump! That isn't funny.
Billy, don't cry.

Dotty Duck can fly by.
Why can Dotty fly?

Dotty is a duck.
That is why she can fly.

Still, Billy will try to fly.
He wants to fly up in the sunny sky.
What will happen?

Freddy Fly is buzzing by.
It is a shame you can't fly, Billy.
But you are a rabbit.

That is why you can't fly.
This is not a contest.
But you can be happy
just the same.

Vi, Mo, and Me

Written by Chantell Brown

Syllable Pattern CV			Vowel Sound of y: /ī/
no	go	be	sky
Mo	he	Vi	my
hi	she	we	by

Vowel Sound of y: /ē/			Consonant ss/s/
silly	sunny	happy	grass pass

High-Frequency Words

said	come	the	want
to	a	I	now
saw	down	was	

153

"No! I will not go!" I said.
"It will not be fun.
It will be silly."

"Mo will come," Mom said.
"Mo likes a picnic in the grass.
He will ask Vi."

"Will Vi and Mo
go now?" I asked.
"I want to see them."

I saw Vi and Mo and the sunny sky.
I yelled at them.
They yelled, "Hi!"

I asked my mom,
"Can I race with
Vi and Mo?"

She said, "Yes, but be safe."
Mo, Vi, and I ran a lot.
Mom did not pass us by!

By the time the sun went
down, it was time to go.
We felt happy.

We Go Fishing

Written by Dylan Demastri

Jenny, Ty, and Bo
will go fishing.
They came to my home.

"Hi, Gwen," yelled Bo.
"We will try to
catch lots of fish."

"Will you be fishing all
day?" I asked.

Jenny asked, "Gwen, will you
fish with us?"

We got poles, and
Ty packed his bag.

Bo made a funny
face as he fished.
"I got a fish!"

Ty rubs his tummy.
He wants a fish fry.

Zing in a Tank

Written by Celia Davos

Consonant Patterns *-ng, -nk*

Zing	tank	honks	wings
stung	bangs	thunk	honking
think	drink	bring	sink
sting	drinking	winked	

Word Family *-ink*

think	drink	sink

Word Family *-onk*

honks
honking

Consonants *zz*

buzz
jazz

High-Frequency Words

a	could	into	the
now	from	to	I

Zing is in a tank.
He honks with his wings.
Buzz, buzz.

I will not let Zing go!
He will be mad at us.
We could get stung.

Zing bangs into the tank.
THUNK!
He is not honking now.

I think Zing needs a drink.
I will bring it from the sink.

I will let Zing go.
Will he try to sting me?

Zing is flying to the dish.
He is drinking.

Buzz, buzz.
Zing honks jazz with his wings.
He is a happy bee.
I think he winked at me.

Inside and Outside

Written by Carole Shannon

Decodable
Practice
Reader
14B

Compound Words

inside	backpack	outside
sunshine	sunblock	treetops
sunset	bedtime	

Consonant Digraph *ch*

checks	lunch	chase

High-Frequency Words

to	do	eats	a
the	for	day	

Pete has lots to do inside.
He checks his fish.
He feeds his fish.

He fills his backpack.
He eats his lunch.
He takes a nap.

Pete can go outside.
Pete has lots to do
in the nice sunshine.

Pete likes to jump.
He can jump rope.
He jumps and jumps.

Pete likes to swim.
He must use sunblock.
He can swim for a while.

Pete likes to fly his kite.
He will chase his kite.
His kite is up in the treetops.

At sunset, Pete must go home.
It is bedtime.
Pete has had a big day!

Pancakes

Written by Sally Hinkley

Compound Words

pancakes   milkshakes   outside
catfish   inside

Plurals -s

pancakes   hats   plates
cups   milkshakes

Consonant Digraph -tch

batch   match   catch

Consonant Patterns -ng, -nk

rang   drank
sink   things
think   trunk
hang

Word Family -ink

sink   think

High-Frequency Words

for   the   wanted   of
new   to   a   put

185

Ben made a batch of pancakes for us.
We like pancakes.

The bell rang on the stove.
Ben gave us hot pancakes.

We drank milkshakes.
We ate and then placed the
cups and plates in the sink.

Then we wanted new things to try.
We will take a long walk outside.

We think we need snug hats
that match.
We see hats that match in that trunk.

We stand by the lake.
No catfish swam by.
We can't catch catfish.

We go inside.
We hang up the hats that match.

Boxes for Flo

Written by Janice Schmidt

Ending -es, Plural -es

boxes	dishes	dresses	sketches	brushes	rushes
pitches	presses	smashes	wishes	fixes	lunches
passes	buses	bunches	fetches	dashes	

Consonants ss

dresses   presses   passes

Long o:o

Flo   go   Bo

High-Frequency Words

where	the	out	to
some	into	a	down
her	for	of	

193

Flo is packing boxes.
She packs dishes and dresses.
She packs sketches and brushes.

Where did the boxes go?
Flo rushes out to get some.

Bo pitches boxes into a bin.
When the top presses down,
it smashes them flat.

Flo wishes she had those boxes.
Will Bo save her some?
Grumpy Bo will not.

Flo fixes homemade lunches.
She gets Bo passes for buses.
That makes Bo happy.

Nice Bo saves bunches
of boxes for Flo.
Thanks, Bo.

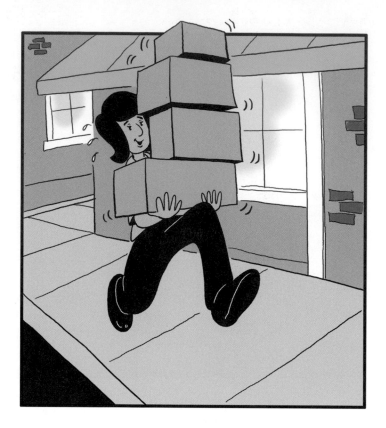

Flo fetches all the boxes.
She dashes back to her packing.

At the Shore

Written by Mary Palmert

I wore my cap from the store.
I got my backpack.
We can go!

We are at a port.
I see ships in the water.
I take a photo of the ships.

Dad and I see a ball game.
The score is six to five.
Who will win the trophy?

We drive to a big fort.
It has a big flag.

It is hot.
We can swim at the shore.
I can run or jump in the waves.

We go for a short walk.
We stop to eat clams and corn.
Dad has more clams than Mom.

We had fun.
But it is time to go!

Going to the Shore

Written by Peter Mok

Dad tosses a big ball.
We got it at the store.
Lin catches it.

We can use it at the shore.
We are going for a short trip.

My bag is packed.
I can't close it.

Mom packs glasses and dishes.
We need them at the shore.

I can take more drink boxes.
I can pick plums or grapes
for my snack.

214

Dad closes the trunk.
We get in.

It is fun to go on a trip.

Hopping Buffy

Written by Nathan Stalworth

Ending -ed, -ing (Double final consonant)

stepped	hopped	hopping
mopped	slipped	dripping
jogged	tripped	stopped
tapped	clapped	tapping
flopped	napped	getting
stepping	running	

Consonants ff

Buffy
huffed
puffed

High-Frequency Words

do	you	could
was	a	good
people	into	look

217

Buffy came.
Do you think she stepped?
No, Buffy hopped!

Buffy could not stop hopping.
She was like a frog.
That was not good.

When Buffy mopped and hopped,
she slipped and fell.
Then she was dripping!

When Buffy jogged,
she could not stop hopping.
Buffy tripped and stopped.

Buffy tapped, and people clapped.
Tapping was a lot like hopping!

Buffy huffed and puffed!
Buffy flopped into bed.
Buffy napped for a while.

At last, Buffy is getting up.
She is stepping and running.
Look! Buffy is not hopping!

Day at the Farm

Written by Jason Dee

Vowels: *r*-Controlled *ar*

farm	barn	hard	harm
cart	yard	smart	bark
dark	star	car	

Consonant Patterns *ng, nk*

Frank   honks   wings   thing

High-Frequency Words

to	they	live
a	the	very
could	look	every
have	from	

Syllable Pattern CV

baby	she
go	

Word Family *-onk*

honks

Cass is going to see Kate
and Frank.
They live on a farm.

Cass sees baby cats in the barn.
She pets them but not very hard.
That could harm them.

Frank takes corn from a cart.
Cass and Kate feed it to hens
and chicks in the yard.
The hens and chicks have wings.

Smart pups bark at sheep.
The pups make them go in the pen.

As it gets dark, Cass, Frank,
and Kate look up.
Every star shines.

Mom honks the car horn.
Cass runs and gets in the car.

Cass likes the farm.
The best thing is
seeing Kate and Frank.

Jogging in the Park

Written by Bill Wright

Vowels: *r*-Controlled *ar*

park   farm   dark
star(s)   cars

Endings -*ed*, -*ing* (Double final consonant)

jogging   jogged   running
slipping   stopped   napping

High-Frequency Words

to   the   around
too   one   a
again   now   are

233

We like to jog and run.
It makes us feel fine.

We go jogging in the park.
We jogged and jogged in
the park.

We go running at the farm.
We ran and ran at the farm.

We go jogging around the track.
We jogged and jogged
around the track.

It is too dark to go jogging.
We see stars in the sky.
One star is slipping.

We go jogging in a race.
The cars stopped for the race.
We jogged and jogged.

We like jogging.
We will jog again, but
now we are napping.

Burt and Gert

Written by Angela Silva

This girl is Fern.
She has a bird.
Her bird is Burt.

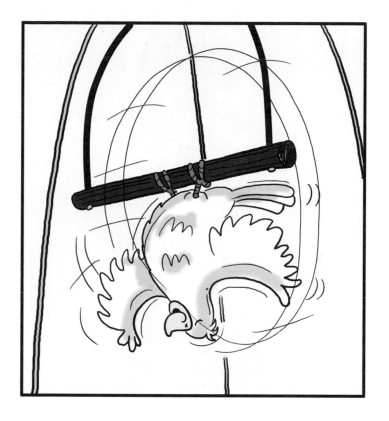

Burt is a good pet.
First he chirps and sings.
Then he twirls on his perch.

This is Herb.
He has a cat.
His cat is Gert.

Gert is a good pet.
First she licks her fur.
Then she curls up and purrs
for a short time.

The friends and their pets
meet on the curb by the store.
What will the pets do?

Gert starts to squirm.
Burt starts to swirl.
This meeting is not going well!

Next time Fern and Herb will meet without pets!

She's Flying!

Written by Lynn Johnson

Contractions

you're   they're

she's   we've

Vowels: *r*-Controlled *ar*

started   stars   hard

Vowels: *r*-Controlled *ir, er, ur*

Gert   bird   curled   her

Endings *-ed, -ing* (Double final consonant)

patted   hopping

hopped

Syllable Pattern CV

baby

he

she

High-Frequency Words

said   to   one

day   the   a

you   around

249

Gert Bird felt like a baby.
"I cannot fly," she said.
She started to cry.

Dad curled his wing around Gert
and patted her wing.
"One day," he said,
"these wings will fly to the stars."

Dad woke Gert the next day.
"You're a big bird.
You can fly!"

Gert began hopping in her nest.
She felt happy.
"I hope I can fly!"

Mom came with Gert and Dad.
"Hop off with those fine feet, Gert.
They're so strong," Mom called.

Gert hopped off the branch.
The wind lifted her up.
"She's flying!" Dad yelled.

"She's flying!" Mom said.
"We've seen Gert try hard."

We've Made Shirts

Written by Karen Finch

Contractions

she's	they're
it's	we've

Vowels: *r*-Controlled *ir, er, ur*

Fern	shirts	stirs
churning	her	turn
twirls	swirls	

Long *i: i*

Vi	hi

High-Frequency Words

a	what	to	the
put	look	said	done

Vi went to see Fern.
Vi said hi to Fern.
Fern makes art.

What art can
Vi make with Fern?
They're going to make fun shirts.

259

First, Fern stirs
in the pink pot.
She's churning it well.

Next, Fern stirs
in the green pot.
Fern makes her shirt.

Vi takes her turn.
Vi twirls her shirt
in the pot with a stick.

"Stop," called Fern.
"It's not done.
Put it back in!"

Look at those swirls!
"We've made cute shirts,"
Vi said.

The Hardest Job

Written by Vivian Fabrice

Comparative Endings *-er, -est*

smaller	smallest	shorter
shortest	fatter	fattest
darker	darkest	smarter
smartest	hotter	
faster	hardest	

Consonants *zz*

Buzz	Muzzy	Fuzzy

High-Frequency Words

every	day	to
the	of	ever

Every day Kirk walks Buzz
to the park.

Sly is smaller than Muzzy.
Perky is smaller still.
Buzz is the smallest of all.

Ike is shorter than Lark.
Tig is shorter still.
Buzz is the shortest of all.

Wink is fatter than Pal.
Curly is fatter still.
Buzz is the fattest of all.

Dee is darker than Ruff.
Sport is darker still.
Buzz is the darkest of all.

Fuzzy is smarter than King.
Jinks is smarter still.
Buzz is the smartest of all.

It is getting hotter.
Buzz walks faster.
This is the hardest job ever!

Where Is My Badge?

Written by Erik Perez

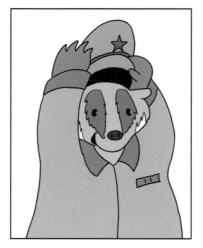

Consonant Pattern -dge

badge   Madge
ledge   edge

Word Family -ink

think   pink
wink

High-Frequency Words

said   to   where   your   I
the   of   find   a   see

273

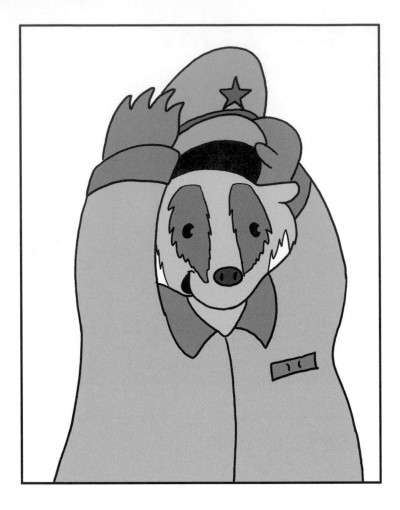

"Let's get my red badge first.
Then we can go,"
Bucky said to Madge.

"Where is my red badge?"
asked Bucky.
"I think I left it on that ledge."

"Is your badge on the edge
of that desk?" Madge asked.
"Did it fall in this trash can?"

"No," said Bucky.
He seemed sadder.
"We can't find my badge."

Madge sat on her bed.
Then she jumped up.
"I see it!" she yelled.

"It is by my pink brush," Madge said.
"Bucky, keep this badge safe.
It is your best badge."

"Thanks, Madge,"
Bucky said with a wink.
He felt glad.

The Fudge Cake

Written by Bill Nieder

Consonant Pattern -dge

fudge   judge
badge

Comparative Endings -er, -est

faster   flattest
hotter   biggest

High-Frequency Words

there   a   the   to
again   said   you

281

There is a prize
for the best cake.
Penny likes to bake.

Penny will bake a cake
to win that prize.
She mixes faster and faster.

Her cake is flat.
"This cake is the flattest.
It will not win."

She made her pan hotter.
Her cake burned.

"I will try again," said Penny.
She did not mix as fast.
She added fudge.

"Did you make this cake?"
asked the judge with the badge.
"It is the biggest cake."

That fudge cake is best.
It wins first prize!